Mini Pies
& mini treats

Publications International, Ltd.

Favorite Brand Name Recipes is a trademark of Publications International, Ltd.

Photography on pages 5, 9, 11, 15, 17, 19, 21, 23, 27, 29, 31, 33, 35, 37, 41, 43, 47, 49, 51, 53, 57, 59, 61, 63, 65, 71, 75, 81, 89 and 105 by PIL Photo Studio North. Photography by David Darian and Christopher Hiltz; prop styling by Jenny Thornton. Recipe testing by Renee Haring, Amanda Kellogg and Jenny Thornton.

Pictured on the front cover: Lemon Cheesecake Tarts *(page 54).*

Pictured on the back cover *(left to right):* Plum-Topped Custard Tartlets *(page 108)* and Rustic Apple Tartlets *(page 12).*

ISBN-13: 978-1-4508-5851-9
ISBN-10: 1-4508-5851-1

Library of Congress Control Number: 2012945152

Manufactured in China.

8 7 6 5 4 3 2 1

Microwave Cooking: Microwave ovens vary in wattage. Use the cooking times as guidelines and check for doneness before adding more time.

Publications International, Ltd.

table of contents

fruit favorites

Raspberry Crumble Mini Pies

crust

1¼ cups all-purpose flour

1½ tablespoons granulated sugar

½ teaspoon salt

¼ cup cold shortening, cubed

6 tablespoons (¾ stick) cold butter, cubed

4 tablespoons ice water

topping

¼ cup all-purpose flour

¼ cup quick or old-fashioned oats

¼ cup packed brown sugar

2 tablespoons melted butter

filling

2 containers (6 ounces each) fresh raspberries

1. For crusts, combine 1¼ cups flour, granulated sugar and salt in food processor; pulse to combine. Add shortening; pulse until blended. Add cold butter; pulse until mixture resembles coarse crumbs. Transfer to medium bowl. Sprinkle with water; use rubber spatula to fold in water until dough comes together. Shape dough into disc. Wrap in plastic wrap; refrigerate 1 hour.

2. For topping, combine ¼ cup flour, oats, brown sugar and melted butter in small bowl; mix well.

3. Preheat oven to 350°F. Roll out dough to ⅛-inch thickness on floured surface (about 15×11-inch rectangle). Cut out circles with 4-inch round cookie cutter. Re-roll scraps of dough to cut out total of 12 circles.

4. Line 12 standard (2½-inch) muffin cups with dough circles, stretching dough as needed and pressing firmly into bottoms and up sides of cups. Fill each crust with ¼ cup raspberries; top with 1 tablespoon oat mixture.

5. Bake 30 to 35 minutes or until raspberries are bubbly. Cool in pan 10 minutes; remove to wire rack to cool completely.

Makes 12 mini pies

tip: If you don't have a 4-inch round cookie cutter, use the rim of a large mug to cut out circles of dough.

Individual Fried Apple-Cranberry Pies

3 tablespoons butter
3 Gala apples (about 12 ounces), peeled and diced
3 tablespoons dried cranberries
3 tablespoons packed brown sugar
1½ tablespoons lemon juice
¾ teaspoon ground cinnamon
¼ teaspoon ground nutmeg
⅛ teaspoon salt
1 package (about 15 ounces) refrigerated pie crusts
Vegetable oil
Powdered sugar

1. For filling, melt butter in large skillet over medium heat. Add apples; cook and stir 8 minutes. Add cranberries, brown sugar, lemon juice, cinnamon, nutmeg and salt; cook and stir 4 minutes or until apples are tender. Transfer to medium bowl; cool 15 minutes.

2. Let crusts stand at room temperature 15 minutes. Heat 2 cups oil in large deep skillet over medium heat to 350°F.

3. Roll out 1 crust into 12½-inch circle on floured surface; cut out 7 circles with 4-inch round cookie cutter. Place generous tablespoon filling on half of each dough circle, leaving ¼-inch border. Dip finger in water and moisten edges of dough. Fold dough over filling, pressing lightly to seal. Dip fork in flour and crimp edges of dough to seal completely.

4. Working in batches, fry pies 1 minute. Turn and fry 1 minute or until lightly browned. Drain on paper towels. Let oil temperature to return to 350°F between batches.

5. Sprinkle with powdered sugar; serve warm or at room temperature.

Makes 14 pies

note: Granny Smith apples can be substituted for Gala apples. Increase brown sugar to ¼ cup and replace lemon juice with water.

variation: These pies can be baked instead of fried. Arrange pies on a parchment paper-lined baking sheet in a preheated 425°F oven; bake 10 minutes or until lightly browned.

Individual Fried Apple-Cranberry Pies

Blueberry Mini Pies

3 cups fresh blueberries *or* 2 packages (16 ounces each) frozen
  blueberries, thawed and drained
1 tablespoons lemon juice
½ cup plus 2 tablespoons sugar
1½ tablespoons quick-cooking tapioca
⅛ teaspoon ground cinnamon
1 package (about 15 ounces) refrigerated pie crusts
2 teaspoons butter, cut into small pieces

1. For filling, place blueberries in large bowl; sprinkle with lemon juice.
Combine sugar, tapioca and cinnamon in small bowl; gently toss with
blueberries until blended.

2. For crusts, preheat oven to 400°F. Line 14 standard (2½-inch) muffin
cups with two 6×1-inch foil strips, criss-crossing strips in bottom of
cups and leaving excess foil overhang for easy removal.

3. Unroll one pie crust on work surface. Cut out 4 circles with 4-inch round
cookie cutter. Re-roll dough scraps and cut out 3 circles. Repeat with
remaining crust to create total of 14 circles. Press dough into prepared
muffin cups; flute edges. Spoon about ¼ cup filling into each crust;
sprinkle evenly with butter.

4. Bake 15 minutes. *Reduce oven temperature to 350°F.* Bake 30 minutes
or until crusts are golden brown. Cool in pan 15 minutes; remove to wire
racks to cool completely. *Makes 14 mini pies*

Blueberry Mini Pies

Tart Cherry Mini Pies

    2 cans (about 14 ounces each) tart cherries, packed in water
 1½ cups sugar
    ¼ cup quick-cooking tapioca
    1 teaspoon ground cinnamon
    1 teaspoon grated lemon peel
    2 tablespoons butter, cut into small pieces
    3 refrigerated pie crusts (1½ [15-ounce] packages)
    1 egg beaten with 1 teaspoon water

1. For filling, drain cherries, reserving ½ cup juice. Place cherries and reserved juice in large bowl. Combine sugar, tapioca, cinnamon and lemon peel in small bowl; gently toss with cherries until blended.

2. For crusts, preheat oven to 425°F. Line 14 standard (2½-inch) muffin cups with two 6×1-inch foil strips, criss-crossing strips in bottom of cups and leaving excess foil overhang for easy removal.

3. Unroll one pie crust on work surface. Cut out 4 circles with 4-inch round cookie cutter. Re-roll dough scraps and cut out 3 circles. Repeat with second crust to create total of 14 circles. Press dough into prepared muffin cups; flute edges. Spoon about ¼ cup filling into each crust; sprinkle evenly with butter.

4. Unroll third crust on work surface; cut into ⅜-inch strips. (Use fluted pastry cutter, if desired.) Arrange strips of dough in lattice design over filling; press ends into bottom crust to seal. Brush top crust lightly with egg mixture.

5. Bake 15 minutes. *Reduce oven temperature to 350°F.* Bake 30 minutes or until filling is bubbly and crusts are golden brown, covering loosely with foil during last 10 minutes of baking to prevent overbrowning. Cool in pans 15 minutes; remove to wire racks. Serve warm or at room temperature.

Makes 14 mini pies

Tart Cherry Mini Pies

Rustic Apple Tartlets

1 tablespoon butter
4 medium Granny Smith, Crispin or other firm-fleshed apples,
    peeled and cut into ¾-inch chunks (about 4 cups)
6 tablespoons granulated sugar
½ teaspoon ground cinnamon
⅛ teaspoon salt
2 teaspoons cornstarch
2 teaspoons lemon juice
1 refrigerated pie crust (half of 15-ounce package)
1 egg, beaten
1 tablespoon coarse or granulated sugar

1. Melt butter in medium saucepan over medium heat; stir in apples, granulated sugar, cinnamon and salt. Cook 10 minutes or until apples are tender, stirring occasionally. Drain apples in colander set over medium bowl; pour liquid back into saucepan. Cook over medium-high heat until liquid is slightly syrupy and reduced by half. Stir in cornstarch; cook 1 minute.

2. Combine apples, lemon juice and cornstarch mixture in medium bowl; toss to coat. Let cool to room temperature.

3. Preheat oven to 425°F. Line large rimmed baking sheet with parchment paper. Unroll pie crust on work surface; cut out 5 circles with 4-inch round cookie cutter. Place dough circles on prepared baking sheet.

4. Divide apples evenly among dough circles, piling apples in center of each circle and leaving ½-inch border. Fold edge of dough up over filling, overlapping and pleating dough as necessary. Press dough gently to adhere to filling. Brush lightly with beaten egg; sprinkle with coarse sugar.

5. Bake about 25 minutes or until crusts are golden brown. Cool on wire rack.   *Makes 5 tartlets*

Rustic Apple Tartlets

Strawberry Rhubarb Mini Pies

Pie Pastry (recipe follows)
1½ cups sugar
½ cup cornstarch
2 tablespoons quick-cooking tapioca
1 tablespoon grated lemon peel
¼ teaspoon ground allspice
4 cups chopped rhubarb (¼-inch pieces)
3 cups chopped strawberries (¼-inch pieces)
1 egg, lightly beaten

1. Prepare Pie Pastry.

2. Preheat oven to 425°F. For filling, combine sugar, cornstarch, tapioca, lemon peel and allspice in large bowl. Add rhubarb and strawberries; toss to coat.

3. Roll out each disc of dough into 5-inch circle (⅛ inch thick) on lightly floured surface. Press dough into eight 4-inch tart pans with removable bottoms; trim excess dough even with edges of pans.

4. Re-roll scraps of dough into 5-inch circles (⅛ inch thick); cut into ¼-inch strips. Spoon about ¾ cup filling into each crust. Arrange strips of dough in lattice design over filling; press ends into bottom crust to seal. Place tart pans on baking sheet.

5. Bake 40 to 45 minutes or until filling is thick and bubbly and crusts are golden brown. Cool on wire rack 15 minutes. Serve warm or at room temperature. *Makes 8 mini pies*

pie pastry: Combine 2½ cups all-purpose flour, 1 teaspoon salt and 1 teaspoon sugar in large bowl. Cut in 1 cup (2 sticks) cold cubed butter with pastry blender or two knives until mixture resembles coarse crumbs. Drizzle ⅓ cup water over flour mixture, 2 tablespoons at a time, stirring just until dough comes together. Divide dough in half; divide each half into 4 pieces. Shape each piece into disc; place discs in resealable food storage bag. Refrigerate 30 minutes.

Strawberry Rhubarb Mini Pies

Apricot Hand Pies

crust

   1¼ cups all-purpose flour

   1½ tablespoons granulated sugar

   ½ teaspoon salt

   ¼ cup cold cream cheese, cubed

   6 tablespoons (¾ stick) cold butter, cubed

   4 tablespoons ice water

filling

   ½ cup chopped walnuts

   ⅓ cup apricot preserves

   ¼ cup golden raisins

   3 tablespoons packed brown sugar

   2 tablespoons granulated sugar

   ½ teaspoon vanilla

   ¼ teaspoon ground cinnamon

   2 tablespoons milk

   2 tablespoons demerara or coarse sugar

1. For crusts, combine flour, 1½ tablespoons granulated sugar and salt in food processor; pulse to combine. Add cream cheese; pulse until blended. Add butter; pulse until mixture resembles coarse crumbs. Transfer to medium bowl. Sprinkle with water; use rubber spatula to fold in water until dough comes together. Shape dough into disc. Wrap in plastic wrap; refrigerate 1 hour.

2. For filling, combine walnuts, preserves, raisins, brown sugar, 2 tablespoons granulated sugar, vanilla and cinnamon in medium bowl; mix well.

3. Preheat oven to 350°F. Line two baking sheets with parchment paper. Roll out dough to ⅛-inch thickness on floured surface (about 15×11-inch rectangle). Cut out circles with 4-inch round cookie cutter. Re-roll scraps of dough to cut out total of 12 circles.

4. Spoon 1 tablespoon filling into center of each circle, leaving ¼-inch border. Fold dough over filling, pressing lightly to seal. Crimp edges of dough with fork to seal completely. Place on prepared baking sheets. Brush pies with milk; sprinkle with demerara sugar.

5. Bake 20 to 25 minutes or until lightly browned. Cool on baking sheets 5 minutes; remove to wire racks to cool completely.

Makes 12 hand pies

Apricot Hand Pies

Apple & Cherry Mini Pies

crust

1¼ cups all-purpose flour

1½ tablespoons granulated sugar

½ teaspoon salt

¼ cup cold shortening, cubed

6 tablespoons (¾ stick) cold butter, cubed

4 tablespoons ice water

filling

⅓ cup dried cherries

2½ tablespoons apple juice

⅓ cup granulated sugar

2 teaspoons cornstarch

1 teaspoon ground cinnamon

3½ cups chopped peeled baking apples such as Jonagold or Golden Delicious

½ teaspoon vanilla

1 egg white, beaten

1 tablespoon demerera or coarse sugar (optional)

1. For crusts, combine flour, 1½ tablespoons granulated sugar and salt in food processor; pulse to combine. Add shortening; pulse until blended. Add butter; pulse until mixture forms coarse crumbs. Transfer to medium bowl. Sprinkle with water; use rubber spatula to fold in water until dough comes together. Shape dough into disc. Wrap in plastic wrap; refrigerate 1 hour.

2. For filling, combine cherries and apple juice in small microwavable bowl; microwave on HIGH 1 minute. Let stand 15 minutes. Combine ⅓ cup granulated sugar, cornstarch and cinnamon in large bowl. Add apples, vanilla and cherry mixture; toss to coat.

3. Preheat oven to 350°F. Roll out dough to ⅛-inch thickness on floured surface (about 15×11-inch rectangle). Cut out circles with 4-inch round cookie cutter. Re-roll scraps of dough to cut out total of 12 circles. Reserve remaining scraps of dough for lattice topping.

4. Line 12 standard (2½-inch) muffin cups with dough circles, stretching dough as needed and pressing firmly into bottoms and up sides of cups. Spoon about ¼ cup filling into each crust.

5. Roll reserved scraps of dough into 1/16-inch-thick square. Cut into 1/4-inch strips; arrange in lattice design over filling. Brush with egg white; sprinkle with demerara sugar, if desired.

6. Bake 25 to 30 minutes or until filling is bubbly and crusts are golden brown. Cool in pan 15 minutes; remove to wire rack to cool completely.

Makes 12 mini pies

tip: If you don't have a 4-inch round cookie cutter, use the rim of a large mug to cut out circles of dough.

Apple & Cherry Mini Pies

Plum Walnut Mini Pies

Pie Pastry (page 21)
Oat Streusel (recipe follows)
8 cups thinly sliced plums, unpeeled
⅓ cup granulated sugar
⅓ cup packed brown sugar
3 to 4 tablespoons all-purpose flour
1 tablespoon honey
½ teaspoon ground cinnamon
¼ teaspoon ground ginger
⅛ teaspoon salt
½ cup candied walnuts

1. Prepare Pie Pastry and Oat Streusel.

2. For filling, place plums in large bowl. Combine granulated sugar, brown sugar, 3 tablespoons flour (use 4 tablespoons if plums are very juicy), honey, cinnamon, ginger and salt in small bowl. Add to plums; gently toss to coat.

3. Preheat oven to 425°F. Roll out each disc of dough into 5-inch circle (⅛ inch thick) on lightly floured surface. Press dough into eight 4-inch tart pans with removable bottoms; trim excess dough even with edges of pans. Spoon about 1 cup filling into each crust; sprinkle with Oat Streusel. Place pies on baking sheet.

4. Bake 15 minutes. *Reduce oven temperature to 350°F.* Sprinkle pies with walnuts. Bake 30 minutes or until filling is bubbly and crusts are golden brown. Cool in pans on wire rack 30 minutes. Serve warm or at room temperature. *Makes 8 mini pies*

oat streusel: Combine ¼ cup all-purpose flour, ¼ cup old-fashioned oats, ¼ cup granulated sugar, ¼ cup packed brown sugar and ⅛ teaspoon salt in medium bowl. Add ¼ cup (½ stick) cubed butter; crumble with fingertips until mixture resembles coarse crumbs.

note: Candied walnuts are available in packages in the baking section of the supermarket; they may also be found in the produce section where salad ingredients are sold.

Pie Pastry

2½ cups all-purpose flour
1 teaspoon salt
6 tablespoons cold shortening, cubed
6 tablespoons (¾ stick) cold butter, cubed
6 to 8 tablespoons ice water
1 teaspoon cider vinegar

1. Combine flour and salt in medium bowl. Cut in shortening and butter with pastry blender or two knives until mixture resembles coarse crumbs.

2. Combine 6 tablespoons water and vinegar in small bowl. Add to flour mixture; mix with fork until dough forms, adding additional water as needed. Divide dough in half; divide each half into four pieces. Shape each piece into disc; place discs in resealable food storage bag. Refrigerate 30 minutes. *Makes pastry for 8 mini (4-inch) pies*

Plum Walnut Mini Pie

Citrus Mini Pies

filling

    6 clementines

    1 lemon

    1 cup granulated sugar

    1 cup packed brown sugar

    4 eggs

crust

    1¼ cups all-purpose flour

    1½ tablespoons granulated sugar

    ½ teaspoon salt

    ¼ cup cold shortening, cubed

    6 tablespoons (¾ stick) cold butter, cubed

    4 tablespoons ice water

1. For filling, wash clementines and lemon; cut into ⅛-inch slices. Remove seeds. Reserve 12 clementine slices; cut all remaining citrus slices into 8 wedges. Combine whole slices, wedges, 1 cup granulated sugar and brown sugar in medium bowl; mix well. Cover and refrigerate overnight.

2. For crusts, combine flour, 1½ tablespoons granulated sugar and salt in food processor; pulse to combine. Add shortening; pulse until blended. Add butter; pulse until mixture resembles coarse crumbs. Transfer to medium bowl. Sprinkle with water; use rubber spatula to fold in water until dough comes together. Shape dough into disc. Wrap in plastic wrap; refrigerate 1 hour.

3. Drain fruit, reserving liquid in large bowl. Remove whole clementine slices and set aside. Add eggs to reserved liquid from fruit; beat with electric mixer at high speed about 3 minutes or until light and fluffy. Gently fold in citrus wedges.

4. Preheat oven to 350°F. Roll out dough to ⅛-inch thickness on floured surface (about 15×11-inch rectangle). Cut out circles with 4-inch round cookie cutter. Re-roll scraps of dough to cut out total of 12 circles.

5. Line 12 standard (2½-inch) muffin cups with dough circles, stretching dough as needed and pressing firmly into bottoms and up sides of cups. Spoon about ¼ cup filling into each crust. Top each pie with clementine slice.

6. Bake 25 to 30 minutes or until set. Cool in pan 10 minutes; remove to wire rack to cool completely. *Makes 12 mini pies*

Citrus Mini Pies

Mini Pies with Three Fillings

1 unbaked 9-inch pie crust
　Apple-Cinnamon Filing, Cherry-Lemon Filling or
　　Chocolate-Banana-Walnut Filling (recipes follow)
1 egg
2 tablespoons water

1. Preheat oven to 425°F. Let dough stand at room temperature
15 minutes. Line baking sheet with parchment paper.

2. Prepare desired filling.

3. Roll out dough into 10- to 12-inch circle on lightly floured surface.
Cut off edges of circle to form square; cut square into four quarters.
Place on prepared baking sheet.

4. Place 2 tablespoons filling on bottom half of each square. Whisk egg
and water in small bowl until blended. Brush egg mixture on edges of
dough. Fold top edge of dough over filling to form rectangular pie; crimp
edges with fork to seal. Freeze 10 minutes.

5. Brush tops of pies with egg mixture. Bake 15 to 17 minutes or until
golden. Cool on wire rack. Drizzle with topping, if desired.

Makes 4 mini pies

apple-cinnamon filling: Prepare pies as directed using ½ cup canned
apple pie filling. Combine 2 tablespoons ground cinnamon and 1 teaspoon
sugar in small bowl. Immediately after baking, brush pies with 1 tablespoon
melted butter; sprinkle with cinnamon-sugar. Serve warm.

cherry-lemon filling: Prepare pies as directed using ½ cup canned cherry
pie filling. Cool slightly. Whisk ¼ cup powdered sugar and 2 teaspoons
lemon juice in small bowl until smooth. Drizzle over pies. Serve warm.

chocolate-banana-walnut filling: Combine 2 mashed peeled bananas,
¼ cup semisweet chocolate chips and ¼ cup chopped walnuts in medium
bowl; mix well. Prepare pies as directed using banana filling. Cool slightly.
Place ¼ cup chocolate chips in small resealable food storage bag;
microwave on LOW (30%) 2 minutes or until melted and smooth.
Drizzle over pies. Serve warm.

Mini Pies with Three Fillings

Strawberry Honey Mini Pies

3 tablespoons honey

½ tablespoon cornstarch

½ teaspoon grated orange peel

½ teaspoon grated lemon peel

½ tablespoon lemon juice

9 medium strawberries, cut into ¼-inch pieces (about 1⅓ cups)

1 refrigerated pie crust (half of 15-ounce package)

½ cup cold whipping cream

3 teaspoons sugar

½ teaspoon vanilla

Fresh mint leaves (optional)

1. For filling, whisk honey, cornstarch, orange peel, lemon peel and lemon juice in medium bowl until smooth. Gently stir in strawberries.

2. For crusts, preheat oven to 350°F. Line 11 nonstick mini (1¾-inch) muffin cups with 5×1-inch foil strips, leaving excess foil overhang for easy removal.

3. Unroll pie crust on work surface. Cut out circles with 3-inch round cookie cutter. Re-roll scraps of dough to cut out total of 11 circles. Press dough into bottoms and up sides of prepared muffin cups. Spoon about 2 tablespoons filling into each crust.

4. Bake about 20 minutes or until filling is bubbly and crusts are golden brown. Cool in pan 15 minutes; remove to wire rack to cool completely.

5. Beat cream, sugar and vanilla in medium bowl with electric mixer at high speed until soft peaks form. Pipe or spoon whipped cream on each pie just before serving; garnish with mint.   *Makes 11 mini pies*

Strawberry Honey Mini Pies

Cranberry Apple Nut Mini Pies

   Rich Pie Pastry (recipe follows)
  1 cup sugar
  3 tablespoons all-purpose flour
  ¼ teaspoon salt
  4 cups sliced peeled tart apples (4 large apples)
  2 cups fresh cranberries
  ½ cup golden raisins
  ½ cup coarsely chopped pecans
  1 tablespoon grated lemon peel
  2 tablespoons butter, cubed
  1 egg, beaten

1. Prepare Rich Pie Pastry.

2. For filling, combine sugar, flour and salt in large bowl. Stir in apples, cranberries, raisins, pecans and lemon peel; mix well.

3. Preheat oven to 425°F. Reserve one disc of dough for lattice topping. Roll out each remaining disc into 5-inch circle (⅛ inch thick) on lightly floured surface. Press dough into seven 4-inch pie plates; trim edges, if necessary. Spoon about 1 cup filling into each crust.

4. Roll out remaining disc of dough to ⅛-inch thickness; cut into ⅜-inch strips. Arrange strips of dough in lattice design over filling; press ends into bottom crust to seal. Brush top crust lightly with beaten egg. Place pie plates on baking sheet.

5. Bake 35 minutes or until apples are tender when pierced with fork and crusts are golden brown. Cool on wire rack 15 minutes. Serve warm or cool completely. *Makes 7 mini pies*

Rich Pie Pastry

  3 cups all-purpose flour
  ½ teaspoon salt
  9 tablespoons cold butter, cubed
  9 tablespoons cold shortening, cubed
  ½ to ¾ cup cold water

1. Combine flour and salt in medium bowl. Cut in butter and shortening with pastry blender or two knives until mixture resembles coarse crumbs.

2. Sprinkle water, 1 tablespoon at a time, over flour mixture, mixing until dough forms. Divide dough in half; divide each half into four pieces. Shape each piece into disc; place discs in resealable food storage bag. Refrigerate 30 minutes.   *Makes pastry for 8 mini (4-inch) pies*

Cranberry Apple Nut Mini Pies

Peach Mini Pies

crust

    ½ cup (1 stick) butter, softened
    ½ cup sugar
    1 egg
    ½ teaspoon vanilla
  1½ cups all-purpose flour
    ¼ teaspoon baking powder

filling

    1 tablespoon plus 1 teaspoon cornstarch
    1 teaspoon ground cinnamon
    ¼ teaspoon ground nutmeg
    ⅛ teaspoon salt
  2½ tablespoons apple juice concentrate
    ½ teaspoon vanilla
  3½ cups chopped peeled fresh peaches or frozen unsweetened
        peaches, thawed and well drained

1. For crusts, beat butter and sugar in large bowl with electric mixer about 2 minutes or until light and fluffy. Add egg and ½ teaspoon vanilla; beat until well blended. Add flour and baking powder; beat just until blended. Wrap in plastic wrap; refrigerate while preparing filling.

2. For filling, combine cornstarch, cinnamon, nutmeg and salt in large bowl. Stir in apple juice concentrate and ½ teaspoon vanilla. Add peaches; toss to coat.

3. Preheat oven to 350°F. Roll out dough to ⅛-inch thickness on floured surface. Cut out circles with 4-inch round cookie cutter. Re-roll scraps of dough to cut out total of 12 circles. Reserve remaining scraps of dough for cutouts, if desired.

4. Line 12 standard (2½-inch) muffin cups with dough circles, stretching dough as needed and pressing firmly into bottoms and up sides of cups. Spoon about ¼ cup filling into each crust.

5. Roll out remaining scraps of dough to ⅛-inch thickness. Cut out shapes with ½-inch cookie cutters. Top each pie with 3 cutouts.

6. Bake 25 to 30 minutes or until filling is bubbly and crusts are golden brown. Cool in pan 15 minutes; remove to wire rack to cool completely.

Makes 12 mini pies

variation: Substitute 1 teaspoon almond extract for the vanilla.

Peach Mini Pies

cool & creamy

Caramelized Lemon Tarts

crust

　　1 cup hazelnuts
　　1 cup graham cracker crumbs (8 to 9 whole crackers)
　　¼ cup powdered sugar
　　7 tablespoons butter, melted

filling

　1½ cups plus 2 tablespoons granulated sugar, divided
　　4 eggs
　⅔ cup whipping cream
　½ cup lemon juice
　　1 vanilla bean, split lengthwise

1. For crusts, preheat oven to 350°F. Spread hazelnuts in single layer on baking sheet. Bake 10 to 12 minutes or until skins begin to flake off. Cool slightly; wrap nuts in heavy kitchen towel and rub to remove as much of skins as possible.

2. Combine toasted hazelnuts, graham cracker crumbs and powdered sugar in food processor; process until finely ground. Add butter; pulse until crumbs are moist and begin to clump.

3. Divide crumb mixture evenly among six 4½-inch tart pans with removable bottoms (3 to 4 tablespoons each); press into bottoms and up sides of pans. Refrigerate crusts while preparing filling.

4. For filling, whisk 1 cup plus 2 tablespoons granulated sugar, eggs, cream and lemon juice in medium bowl until blended. Scrape in seeds from vanilla bean; mix well. Place chilled crusts on baking sheet; pour filling into crusts.

5. Bake 25 to 30 minutes or until filling is set. Cool completely on wire rack; refrigerate until cold.

6. Preheat broiler. Sprinkle 1 tablespoon granulated sugar over each tart. Broil about 1 minute or until golden brown. Refrigerate 10 to 15 minutes before serving. *Makes 6 tarts*

Banana Cream Mini Pies

crust

1¼ cups sifted all-purpose flour
1 teaspoon salt
¾ teaspoon baking powder
5 tablespoons cold lard or shortening, cubed
5 tablespoons cold butter, cubed
3 to 4 tablespoons cold whole milk

filling

¾ cup sugar
9 tablespoons cornstarch
½ teaspoon salt
4 cups whole milk
3 egg yolks
2 teaspoons vanilla
4 bananas, divided
1 teaspoons lemon juice
Whipped cream
Ground cinnamon (optional)

1. For crusts, sift flour, 1 teaspoon salt and baking powder into medium bowl. Cut in lard and butter with pastry blender or two knives until mixture resembles coarse crumbs. Add milk, 1 tablespoon at a time, tossing quickly with fork until mixture holds together. Turn out onto lightly floured surface; shape dough into disc. Wrap in plastic wrap; refrigerate at least 1 hour or overnight. (If refrigerated for several hours or overnight, let dough stand at room temperature 30 minutes before using.)

2. Divide dough into 4 pieces. Roll out each piece into 6½-inch circle (about ⅛ inch thick) on lightly floured surface. Gently press dough into four 5-inch pie plates, pleating dough as necessary. Trim and crimp edges with fork; prick bottom of dough with fork. Refrigerate 30 minutes.

3. Preheat oven to 400°F. Line each crust with foil or parchment paper; fill with pie weights or dried beans. Place pie plates on baking sheet; bake 15 minutes. Remove pie weights and foil; bake 5 to 7 minutes or until crusts are golden brown. Cool on wire rack.

4. For filling, combine sugar, cornstarch and ½ teaspoon salt in medium saucepan. Whisk 4 cups milk and egg yolks in medium bowl; slowly stir into sugar mixture. Cook and stir over medium heat until thickened. Boil 1 minute, stirring constantly. Remove from heat; stir in vanilla.

5. Slice 3 bananas; toss with lemon juice. Layer bananas on bottom and up side of each crust. Pour filling over bananas; immediately cover with waxed paper. Refrigerate 2 hours or until ready to serve.

6. Just before serving, slice remaining banana. Top each pie with whipped cream and banana slice. Sprinkle with cinnamon, if desired.

Makes 4 mini pies

Banana Cream Mini Pie

Pumpkin Chiffon Mini Pies

crust

3 cups gingersnap cookie crumbs*
½ cup granulated sugar
1 teaspoon salt
¾ cup (1½ sticks) butter, melted

filling

2 cups canned solid-pack pumpkin
1 can (12 ounces) evaporated milk
¾ cup packed brown sugar
2 eggs
1¼ teaspoons ground cinnamon
½ teaspoon salt
½ teaspoon ground nutmeg
½ teaspoon ground ginger
¼ teaspoon ground cloves
Whipped cream (optional)

About 60 (2-inch) gingersnap cookies are needed to make 3 cups of crumbs. Use food processor or place cookies in large resealable food storage bag and crush with rolling pin.

1. Preheat oven to 425°F. For crusts, combine gingersnap crumbs, granulated sugar and 1 teaspoon salt in medium bowl; mix well. Stir in butter until well blended.

2. Divide crumb mixture evenly among eight 5-inch pie plates (about 3½ tablespoons each); press into bottoms and up sides of pie plates. Place pie plates on baking sheet.

3. For filling, whisk pumpkin, evaporated milk, brown sugar, eggs, cinnamon, ½ teaspoon salt, nutmeg, ginger and cloves in medium bowl until well blended. Pour about ½ cup filling into each crust.

4. Bake 10 minutes. *Reduce oven temperature to 350°F.* Bake 25 to 30 minutes or until toothpick inserted into centers of pies comes out clean. Cool completely on wire racks. Serve at room temperature or chilled. Top with whipped cream, if desired.   *Makes 8 mini pies*

Pumpkin Chiffon Mini Pies

Frozen Piña Colada Pies

¾ cup sweetened condensed milk
¼ cup Key lime or regular lime juice
2 egg yolks*
8 mini graham cracker crusts
1 cup milk
⅓ cup coconut cream instant pudding and pie filling mix
   (half of 4-serving size package)
1 cup thawed frozen whipped topping
½ cup shredded coconut, toasted (see Tip)
Lime peel twists (optional)

Since eggs are not cooked in this recipe, you may substitute ½ cup pasteurized eggs for the egg yolks if you prefer to avoid raw eggs.

1. Whisk sweetened condensed milk, lime juice and egg yolks in small bowl until well blended. Spoon about 2 tablespoons mixture into each crust.

2. Whisk milk and pudding mix in medium bowl until well blended. Whisk in whipped topping. Spoon ¼ cup pudding mixture over lime layer in each crust.

3. Freeze about 3 hours or until firm. Sprinkle with coconut; garnish with lime peel.   *Makes 8 mini pies*

tip

To toast coconut, cook and stir the coconut in a small nonstick skillet over medium heat 1 to 2 minutes or until lightly browned. Immediately remove from the skillet to prevent burning.

Frozen Piña Colada Pies

Raisin Custard Mini Pies

crust

- 1¼ cups all-purpose flour
- 1½ tablespoons sugar
- ½ teaspoon salt
- ¼ cup cold shortening, cubed
- 6 tablespoons (¾ stick) cold butter, cubed
- 4 tablespoons ice water

filling

- 2 cup whipping cream
- ⅔ cup sugar
- 3 eggs
- 1 egg yolk
- ¼ teaspoon salt
- 2 tablespoons vanilla
- ¼ cup golden raisins

1. For crusts, combine flour, 1½ tablespoons sugar and ½ teaspoon salt in food processor; pulse to combine. Add shortening; pulse until blended. Add butter; pulse until mixture resembles coarse crumbs. Transfer to medium bowl. Sprinkle with water; use rubber spatula to fold in water until dough comes together. Shape dough into disc. Wrap in plastic wrap; refrigerate 1 hour.

2. For filling, bring cream to a simmer in medium saucepan over medium heat. Whisk ⅔ cup sugar, eggs, egg yolk and ¼ teaspoon salt in medium bowl until blended. Slowly pour hot cream into egg mixture, whisking until well blended. Return mixture to saucepan; cook over medium-low heat about 10 minutes or until thickened, stirring constantly. Remove from heat; stir in vanilla.

3. Preheat oven to 350°F. Roll out dough to ⅛-inch thickness on floured surface (about 15×11-inch rectangle). Cut out circles with 4-inch round cookie cutter. Re-roll scraps of dough to cut out total of 12 circles.

4. Line 12 standard (2½-inch) muffin cups with dough circles, stretching dough as needed and pressing firmly into bottoms and up sides of cups. Place 1 teaspoon raisins in each crust; pour about ¼ cup filling over raisins.

5. Bake 20 to 25 minutes or until set. Cool in pan 10 minutes; remove to wire rack to cool completely. *Makes 12 mini pies*

Raisin Custard Mini Pies

Cranberry Meringue Mini Pies

crust

  2½ cups all-purpose flour

   3 tablespoons sugar

   1 teaspoon grated orange peel

   ½ teaspoon grated lemon peel

   ⅛ teaspoon salt

   1 cup (2 sticks) cold butter, cubed

   2 egg yolks

   ¼ cup ice water

filling

   1 package (12 ounces) fresh cranberries, divided

  1¾ cups water, divided

  1½ cups sugar, divided

  1½ teaspoons grated orange peel

   ½ teaspoon grated lemon peel

   ¼ teaspoon salt

   ⅛ teaspoon ground cinnamon

   ⅛ teaspoon ground nutmeg

   ¼ cup fresh orange juice

   3 tablespoons cornstarch

   3 egg whites

   ⅛ teaspoon cream of tartar

1. For crusts, combine flour, 3 tablespoons sugar, 1 teaspoon orange peel, ½ teaspoon lemon peel and ⅛ teaspoon salt in food processor; pulse to combine. Add butter; pulse until mixture resembles coarse crumbs. Beat egg yolks and ¼ cup water in small bowl. Add to food processor with motor running; process about 30 seconds or just until dough holds together. Shape dough into two discs. Wrap in plastic wrap; refrigerate 30 minutes or until firm.

2. Preheat oven to 375°F. Divide dough into 12 pieces. Roll out each piece into 4-inch circle on lightly floured surface (about ⅛ inch thick). Press dough into bottoms and up sides of 12 standard (2½-inch) muffin cups, pleating dough as necessary. Trim and crimp edges with fork or flute. Prick bottoms with fork; freeze 15 minutes. Line each crust with parchment paper or foil; fill with pie weights or dried beans. Bake 15 minutes. Remove pie weights and parchment paper; bake 5 to 7 minutes or until edges are golden brown. Cool in pan 5 minutes; remove to wire rack to cool completely.

3. For filling, bring 2 cups cranberries, 1½ cups water and 1 cup sugar to a boil in medium saucepan. Reduce heat to medium-low; simmer about 5 minutes or until cranberries burst, stirring occasionally. Strain mixture, reserving liquid. (You should have about 1¾ cups.) Discard solids.

4. Pour liquid back into saucepan. Add ¼ cup sugar, 1½ teaspoons orange peel, ½ teaspoon lemon peel, ¼ teaspoon salt, cinnamon, nutmeg and remaining cranberries; bring to a boil. Reduce heat to medium-low; simmer about 3 minutes, stirring occasionally.

5. Combine orange juice, cornstarch and remaining ¼ cup water in small bowl until well blended. Whisk into cranberry mixture. Bring to a boil, stirring constantly. Cook and stir 1 minute. Pour filling evenly into prepared crusts; refrigerate at least 1 hour or until set.

6. Preheat broiler. Place pies on baking sheet. Combine egg whites and remaining ¼ cup sugar in medium bowl of electric mixer. Set bowl over simmering water; whisk until sugar is dissolved and mixture is hot. Beat with electric mixer at medium speed until foamy. Add cream of tartar; beat at high speed until glossy peaks form. Spoon meringue into piping bag; pipe onto pies. Broil 30 seconds to 1 minute or until meringue is lightly browned.   *Makes 12 mini pies*

Cranberry Meringue Mini Pie

Mini Peppermint Cheesecake Pies

2 packages (8 ounces each) cream cheese, softened
1 cup powdered sugar, sifted
1 teaspoon peppermint extract
1 cup cold whipping cream
3 to 4 drops red food coloring
25 peppermint candies (about 4 ounces), crushed, divided
6 mini graham cracker crusts

1. Beat cream cheese, powdered sugar and peppermint extract in large bowl with electric mixer at medium speed until smooth.

2. Beat cream and food coloring in medium bowl with electric mixer at high speed until stiff peaks form. Fold whipped cream and three fourths of crushed peppermints into cream cheese mixture.

3. Divide mixture evenly among pie crusts, mounding in centers. Refrigerate 1 hour or until ready to serve.

4. Sprinkle with remaining crushed peppermints. *Makes 6 servings*

tip

These pies may be made up to 2 days in advance,
but don't sprinkle with the crushed candy until just
before you are ready to serve them.

Mini Peppermint Cheesecake Pies

Peanut Butter Mini Pies

filling

⅔ cup sugar

3 tablespoons cornstarch

½ teaspoon salt

2½ cups whole milk

3 egg yolks, beaten

½ cup creamy peanut butter

1 teaspoon vanilla

⅔ cup chopped mini peanut butter cups

crust

2 cups all-purpose flour

1 teaspoon baking soda

½ teaspoon salt

2 cups sugar

¾ cup (1½ sticks) butter, softened

¼ cup creamy peanut butter

⅔ cup unsweetened cocoa powder

2 eggs

2 teaspoons vanilla

Chocolate Ganache (page 47)

1. For filling, combine ⅔ cup sugar, cornstarch and ½ teaspoon salt in large saucepan. Stir in milk and egg yolks until well blended. Bring to a boil over medium heat; cook until thickened, stirring occasionally. Remove from heat; stir in ½ cup peanut butter and 1 teaspoon vanilla until smooth. Transfer to medium bowl; cover and refrigerate 1 hour.

2. For crusts, preheat oven to 350°F. Combine flour, baking soda and ½ teaspoon salt in medium bowl. Beat 2 cups sugar, butter and ¼ cup peanut butter in large bowl with electric mixer about 2 minutes or until light and fluffy. Add cocoa, eggs and 2 teaspoons vanilla; beat until well blended. Gradually add flour mixture; beat until blended.

3. Spoon 2 teaspoons dough into 48 mini (1¾-inch) muffin cups. Press thumb into center of dough to create indentation. Bake 7 minutes. Remove from oven; press end of wooden spoon into centers to create crusts. Bake 1 minute; repeat pressing and baking if necessary to hold shape of crusts. Cool in pans 10 minutes; remove to wire racks to cool completely.

4. Stir chopped peanut butter cups into filling. Spoon about 1½ tablespoons filling into each crust. Cover and refrigerate at least 4 hours.

5. Prepare Chocolate Ganache; drizzle over pies.   *Makes 8 servings*

chocolate ganache: Place ¼ cup whole milk in medium microwavable bowl; microwave on HIGH 1 minute or until boiling. Stir in 4 ounces semisweet chocolate chips; stir until chocolate is melted. Let stand 5 minutes to thicken slightly.

Peanut Butter Mini Pies

Vanilla Pudding Mini Pies

crust

>   3 cups graham cracker crumbs
>   ⅔ cup butter, melted
>   ½ cup packed brown sugar
>   ¼ teaspoon ground nutmeg

filling

>   3 egg yolks
>   ⅓ cup granulated sugar
>   3 tablespoons plus 1 teaspoon cornstarch
>   ¼ teaspoon salt
>   3 cups whole milk
>   2 tablespoons butter
> 1½ teaspoons vanilla

1. For crusts, preheat oven to 350°F. Combine graham cracker crumbs, melted butter, brown sugar and nutmeg in medium bowl; mix well. Spoon about ¼ cup mixture into each of twelve 8-ounce ramekins or custard cups; press firmly into bottoms and up sides to completely cover inside of each ramekin.

2. Bake 10 to 15 minutes or until golden brown. Cool completely on wire racks.

3. For filling, beat egg yolks in medium bowl with electric mixer about 3 minutes or until light and fluffy. Combine granulated sugar, cornstarch and salt in medium saucepan; whisk in milk until blended. Cook and stir over medium heat until mixture begins to bubble and thicken. Reduce heat to low; cook 2 minutes, stirring constantly. Remove from heat.

4. Stir ¼ cup hot milk mixture into beaten egg yolks; slowly add egg yolk mixture to saucepan, whisking constantly. Bring to a simmer; cook and stir 1 minute. Remove from heat, stir in butter and vanilla. Cool 15 minutes, stirring occasionally. Spoon about ¼ cup filling into each crust.

5. Cover each pie with plastic wrap to prevent skin from forming. Refrigerate at least 1 hour before serving.   *Makes 12 mini pies*

Vanilla Pudding Mini Pies

Cranberry Sour Cream Mini Pies

crust

> 1¼ cups all-purpose flour
> 1½ tablespoons sugar
> ½ teaspoon salt
> ¼ cup cold shortening, cubed
> 6 tablespoons (¾ stick) cold butter, cubed
> 4 tablespoons ice water

filling

> 2 eggs
> 2 egg yolks
> 1½ cups low-fat sour cream
> 1 cup sugar
> ½ teaspoon vanilla
> ¼ teaspoon salt
> 1 cup sweetened dried cranberries

1. For crusts, combine flour, 1½ tablespoons sugar and ½ teaspoon salt in food processor; pulse to combine. Add shortening; pulse until blended. Add butter; pulse until mixture forms coarse crumbs. Transfer to medium bowl. Sprinkle with water; use rubber spatula to fold in water until dough comes together. Shape dough into disc. Wrap in plastic wrap; refrigerate 1 hour.

2. For filling, whisk eggs and egg yolks in large bowl until blended. Stir in sour cream, 1 cup sugar, vanilla and ¼ teaspoon salt until well blended. Stir in cranberries.

3. Preheat oven to 350°F. Roll out dough to ⅛-inch thickness on floured surface (about 15×11-inch rectangle). Cut out circles with 4-inch round cookie cutter. Re-roll scraps of dough to cut out total of 12 circles.

4. Line 12 standard (2½-inch) muffin cups with dough circles, stretching dough as needed and pressing firmly into bottoms and up sides of cups. Spoon about ¼ cup filling into each crust.

5. Bake 20 to 25 minutes or until set. Cool in pan 10 minutes; remove to wire rack to cool completely. Chill pies before serving.

Makes 12 mini pies

note: Do not substitute full-fat or fat-free sour cream in this recipe.

Cranberry Sour Cream Mini Pies

Frozen Cappuccino Mini Pies

4 ounces cream cheese, softened
⅔ cup sweetened condensed milk
¼ cup chocolate syrup
½ tablespoon instant coffee granules
½ tablespoon hot water
¾ cup thawed frozen whipped topping
8 mini graham cracker crusts
3 tablespoons chopped pecans, toasted*
Additional chocolate syrup

To toast pecans, spread in single layer in heavy skillet. Cook over medium heat 1 to 2 minutes or until lightly browned, stirring frequently. Remove from skillet immediately. Cool before using.

1. For filling, beat cream cheese in large bowl with electric mixer at medium speed 2 to 3 minutes or until light and fluffy. Add sweetened condensed milk and ¼ cup chocolate syrup; beat at low speed until well blended.

2. Dissolve coffee powder in hot water in small bowl. Slowly stir into cream cheese mixture. Fold in whipped topping until blended.

3. Spoon about ⅓ cup filling into each crust; sprinkle with pecans. Cover and freeze overnight.

4. Let pies stand in refrigerator 10 to 15 minutes before serving. Drizzle with additional chocolate syrup.   *Makes 8 mini pies*

Frozen Cappuccino Mini Pies

Lemon Cheesecake Tarts

crust

> **Basic Short Dough (page 107)**
> 2 teaspoons grated lemon peel

filling

> 1 package (8 ounces) cream cheese, softened
> ¼ cup sugar
> ½ cup prepared lemon curd
> Lemon peel (optional)
> Fresh mint leaves (optional)

1. For crusts, prepare Basic Short Dough, adding 2 teaspoons lemon peel to butter and sugar mixture. Divide dough into half; shape each half into disc. Wrap in plastic wrap; refrigerate at least 1 hour or until firm.

2. Remove dough from refrigerator; let stand 5 minutes. Lightly spray 48 mini (1¾-inch) muffin cups with nonstick cooking spray.

3. Roll out half of dough to ⅛-inch thickness on lightly floured surface. Cut out circles with 2½-inch fluted round cookie cutter. Place in prepared muffin cups, pressing dough into bottoms and up sides of cups and sealing any cracks. Repeat with remaining dough. Re-roll dough scraps once. Refrigerate at least 30 minutes before baking.

4. Preheat oven to 375°F. Prick holes in bottom of each crust with fork. Bake 10 to 12 minutes or until golden brown. Cool completely in pans on wire rack.

5. For filling, beat cream cheese and sugar in medium bowl with electric mixer at medium speed until creamy. Stir in lemon curd until blended.

6. Spoon about 2 teaspoons filling into each crust. Cover and refrigerate at least 2 hours before serving. Garnish with additional lemon peel and mint. Store covered in refrigerator.   *Makes 4 dozen tarts*

Lemon Cheesecake Tarts

Grasshopper Mini Pies

crust

22 chocolate wafer cookies
3 tablespoons sugar
¼ cup (½ stick) butter, melted

filling

1 cup whole milk
¼ teaspoon salt
3 egg yolks
2 tablespoons cornstarch
6 ounces white chocolate, chopped
2 tablespoons butter
2 tablespoons crème de menthe
2 tablespoons light crème de cacao
¾ cup cold whipping cream
Chocolate curls or grated chocolate (optional)

1. For crusts, combine cookies and sugar in food processor; process until finely ground. Add melted butter; process just until mixture holds together. Divide crumb mixture evenly among six 6-ounce ramekins (3 to 4 tablespoons each); press into bottoms and up sides of ramekins. Place in freezer while preparing filling.

2. For filling, bring milk and salt to a simmer in medium heavy saucepan. Whisk egg yolks and cornstarch in medium bowl until well blended. Gradually whisk in hot milk until blended. Return mixture to saucepan; cook and stir over medium-low heat 2 to 3 minutes or until thickened. Remove from heat; whisk in white chocolate and 2 tablespoons butter until smooth.

3. Transfer filling to medium bowl; whisk in crème de menthe and crème de cacao. Set bowl inside larger bowl of ice water; let stand about 30 minutes or until thickened and cold, stirring frequently.

4. Beat cream in medium bowl with electric mixer at high speed until stiff peaks form. Stir one third of whipped cream into cold filling. Fold in remaining whipped cream until well blended.

5. Divide filling evenly among frozen crusts. Freeze at least 3 hours or up to 2 days. Garnish with chocolate curls. *Makes 6 mini pies*

Grasshopper Mini Pies

Sweet Ricotta Mini Pies

filling

½ cup whole milk

2 strips (3×1-inch) orange peel

3 tablespoons granulated sugar

1 egg yolk

1 tablespoons cornstarch

⅛ teaspoon salt

½ teaspoon vanilla

8 ounces ricotta cheese

¾ teaspoon fresh orange juice

1 tablespoon candied orange peel, finely chopped

1 tablespoon candied lemon peel, finely chopped

crust

2¼ cups all-purpose flour

6 tablespoons granulated sugar

½ teaspoon salt

1 cup (2 sticks) cold butter, cubed

½ teaspoon grated orange peel

2 egg yolks

2 tablespoons ice water

1 egg beaten with 1 tablespoon water

Powdered sugar

1. For filling, bring milk and orange peel strips to a simmer in medium heavy saucepan. Whisk 3 tablespoons granulated sugar, 1 egg yolk, cornstarch and ⅛ teaspoon salt in medium bowl until well blended. Gradually whisk in hot milk. Return mixture to saucepan; bring to a boil over medium heat, whisking constantly. Boil 1 minute. Remove from heat; stir in vanilla. Transfer filling to medium bowl; cover surface directly with plastic wrap or parchment paper. Refrigerate at least 1 hour or until cold.

2. Remove orange peel strips from filling. Place ricotta in food processor; process until smooth. Whisk ricotta into cold filling until blended. Stir in orange juice and candied orange and lemon peels. Refrigerate until ready to use.

3. For crusts, butter 12 nonstick standard (2½-inch) muffin cups and top surface of muffin pan.

4. Combine flour, 6 tablespoons granulated sugar and ½ teaspoon salt in food processor; pulse until combined. Add butter and grated orange peel; pulse until mixture resembles coarse crumbs. Add 2 egg yolks and ice water; pulse until dough begins to form large clumps. Turn out onto work surface; press together to form a ball.

5. Press 2 tablespoons dough into bottom and up side of each prepared muffin cup. Crimp edges of dough with fork or flute. Refrigerate at least 30 minutes or until firm.

6. Roll out remaining dough to ⅛-inch thickness between two pieces of parchment paper. Remove top piece of parchment; cut dough into ¼- to ½-inch strips.

7. Preheat oven to 350°F. Place oven rack in center position. Spoon scant 2 tablespoons filling into each crust; smooth top. Trim strips of dough to fit tops of pies; arrange over filling as desired. Brush edges of dough and dough strips with beaten egg mixture.

8. Bake 25 to 30 minutes or until filling is puffed and beginning to crack and crusts are golden brown. Cool in pan 10 minutes; remove to wire rack to cool completely. Sprinkle with powdered sugar. Serve at room temperature. *Makes 12 mini pies*

Sweet Ricotta Mini Pies

Key Lime Mini Pies

8 mini graham cracker crusts
1 egg white, lightly beaten
1 can (14 ounces) sweetened condensed milk
4 egg yolks
3 to 4 teaspoons grated lime peel (about 2 medium limes)
½ cup plus 2 tablespoons lime juice (about 5 medium limes)
   Additional grated lime peel (optional)

1. Preheat oven to 350°F. Place crusts on baking sheet; brush lightly with egg white. Bake 5 minutes.

2. For filling, whisk sweetened condensed milk, egg yolks and lime peel in medium bowl until well blended. Whisk in lime juice (mixture will thicken slightly). Pour filling into prepared crusts on baking sheet.

3. Bake 10 minutes. Remove to wire rack to cool completely. Cover and refrigerate at least 2 hours. Garnish with additional lime peel.

Makes 8 mini pies

Pretty Pink Pies

1 small ripe banana, sliced
6 mini graham cracker crusts
2 tablespoons chocolate ice cream topping
2 containers (6 ounces each) strawberry yogurt
6 mini pastel marshmallows
6 medium fresh strawberries, cut into wedges

1. Arrange banana slices in bottoms of pie crusts. Drizzle with chocolate topping; top with yogurt.

2. Place one marshmallow in center of each pie. Arrange strawberry wedges around marshmallow to resemble flower. Serve immediately or cover and refrigerate up to 4 hours.

Makes 6 mini pies

Key Lime Mini Pies

Sweet Potato-Honey Mini Pies

1 can (29 ounces) cut-up sweet potatoes
2 eggs
⅔ cup honey
2 tablespoons butter, melted
¾ teaspoon ground cinnamon
½ teaspoon salt
½ teaspoon ground ginger
¼ teaspoon ground cloves
1 cup whole milk
1 package (about 15 ounces) refrigerated pie crusts
Whipped cream (optional)
Additional ground cinnamon (optional)

1. For filling, drain sweet potatoes, reserving 2 tablespoons syrup. Place sweet potatoes and syrup in food processor; pulse until smooth. Measure 2½ cups, reserving any remaining purée for another use.

2. Whisk eggs in large bowl. Whisk in sweet potato purée, honey, butter, cinnamon, salt, ginger and cloves until well blended. Whisk in milk.

3. For crusts, preheat oven to 400°F. Line 14 standard (2½-inch) muffin cups with two 6×1-inch foil strips, criss-crossing strips in bottom of cups and leaving excess foil overhang for easy removal.

4. Unroll one pie crust on work surface. Cut out 4 circles with 4-inch round cookie cutter. Re-roll dough scraps and cut out 3 circles. Repeat with remaining crust to create total of 14 circles. Press dough into prepared muffin cups; flute edges. Spoon about ¼ cup filling into each crust.

5. Bake 15 minutes. *Reduce oven temperature to 350°F.* Bake 35 minutes or until filling is puffed. Cool in pans 15 minutes; remove to wire racks to cool completely. Serve at room temperature or chilled; top with whipped cream and sprinkle with additional cinnamon, if desired.

Makes 14 mini pies

Sinfully Rich Chocolate Pies

filling

- 6 egg yolks
- 6 tablespoons sugar
- 2 tablespoons plus 1 teaspoon cornstarch
- ¼ teaspoon salt
- 2 cups whole milk
- 6 ounces bittersweet or semisweet chocolate, chopped
- 1½ tablespoons crème de cacao
- ½ cup coarsely chopped toasted almonds*
- Whipped cream
- Slivered almonds (optional)

crust

- 2 cups graham cracker crumbs
- 3 tablespoons sugar
- ½ cup (1 stick) butter, melted

*To toast almonds, spread in single layer on baking sheet. Bake in preheated 375°F oven 4 to 6 minutes or until golden brown, stirring frequently.

1. For filling, whisk egg yolks, 6 tablespoons sugar, cornstarch and salt in medium bowl until well blended. Bring milk to a simmer in medium heavy saucepan over medium heat. Slowly pour milk into egg yolk mixture, whisking constantly. Return mixture to saucepan; whisk about 2½ minutes or until custard boils and thickens.

2. Remove from heat; whisk in chopped chocolate and crème de cacao until chocolate is melted and mixture is smooth. Stir in chopped almonds. Transfer custard to medium bowl; place plastic wrap directly on surface. Refrigerate at least 2 hours or until cold.

3. For crusts, preheat oven to 375°F. Combine graham cracker crumbs and 3 tablespoons sugar in medium bowl; stir in butter until well blended. Divide crumb mixture evenly among eight 6-ounce custard cups (about 4½ tablespoons each); press into bottoms and up sides to completely cover inside of each cup.

4. Place cups on baking sheet; bake 8 to 10 minutes or until crusts are set and lightly browned. Cool on wire rack.

5. Spoon chocolate custard into crusts. Top with whipped cream and slivered almonds, if desired. *Makes 8 mini pies*

Sinfully Rich Chocolate Pies

Maple-Sweet Potato Cheesecake Mini Pies

1 package (8 ounces) cream cheese, softened
½ cup vanilla yogurt
1 can (16 ounces) sweet potatoes, drained and mashed (see Tip)
½ cup pure maple syrup
1 teaspoon vanilla
½ teaspoon ground cinnamon
¼ teaspoon ground cloves
1 egg
1 egg white
12 mini graham cracker crusts
12 pecan halves

1. Preheat oven to 350°F. Beat cream cheese in large bowl with electric mixer at medium speed until creamy. Add yogurt; beat until smooth. Add mashed sweet potatoes, maple syrup, vanilla, cinnamon and cloves; beat until smooth. Beat in egg and egg white until blended.

2. Spoon about ⅓ cup sweet potato mixture into each crust. Top with pecan half. Place filled crusts on large baking sheet.

3. Bake 30 to 35 minutes or until set and knife inserted into centers comes out clean. Cool 1 hour on wire rack. Chill before serving.

Makes 12 mini pies

tip

Mashing sweet potatoes by hand produces pie filling
with a somewhat coarse texture. For a smoother texture,
process sweet potatoes in a food processor.

Maple-Sweet Potato Cheesecake Mini Pies

Pumpkin Tartlets

1 refrigerated pie crust (half of 15-ounce package)
1 can (15 ounces) solid-pack pumpkin
⅔ cup granulated sugar
¼ cup milk
1 egg
¾ teaspoon ground cinnamon
½ teaspoon vanilla
⅛ teaspoon salt
⅛ teaspoon ground nutmeg
   Dash ground allspice
1½ cups whipped topping

1. For crusts, preheat oven to 425°F. Spray 12 standard (2½-inch) muffin cups with nonstick cooking spray.

2. Unroll pie crust on work surface. Cut out 12 circles with 2½-inch biscuit cutter; discard scraps. Press one circle into each prepared muffin cup.

3. For filling, whisk pumpkin, sugar, milk, egg, cinnamon, vanilla, salt, nutmeg and allspice in medium bowl until well blended. Spoon about 2 tablespoons pumpkin mixture into each crust.

4. Bake 10 minutes. *Reduce oven temperature to 325°F.* Bake 12 to 15 minutes or until knife inserted into centers comes out clean. Remove to wire rack; cool completely. Top with whipped topping just before serving. *Makes 12 tartlets*

Pumpkin Tartlet

Chocolate Chip Cookie Mini Pies

crust

1¼ cups all-purpose flour

1½ tablespoons granulated sugar

½ teaspoon salt

¼ cup cold shortening, cubed

6 tablespoons (¾ stick) cold butter, cubed

4 tablespoons ice water

filling

¾ cup (1½ sticks) butter, softened

½ cup granulated sugar

½ cup packed brown sugar

½ teaspoon vanilla

2 eggs

¾ cup all-purpose flour

1 cup (6 ounces) semisweet chocolate chips

½ cup chopped pecans

1. For crusts, combine 1¼ cups flour, 1½ tablespoons granulated sugar and salt in food processor; pulse to combine. Add shortening; pulse until blended. Add cold butter; pulse until mixture forms coarse crumbs. Transfer to medium bowl. Sprinkle with water; use rubber spatula to fold in water until dough comes together. Shape dough into disc. Wrap in plastic wrap; refrigerate 1 hour.

2. For filling, beat softened butter, ½ cup granulated sugar, brown sugar and vanilla in large bowl with electric mixer at medium speed until light and fluffy. Add eggs; beat until well blended. Beat in flour just until blended. Stir in chocolate chips and nuts.

3. Preheat oven to 350°F. Roll out dough to ⅛-inch thickness on floured surface (about 15×11-inch rectangle). Cut out circles with 4-inch round cookie cutter. Re-roll scraps of dough to cut out total of 12 circles.

4. Line 12 standard (2½-inch) muffin cups with dough circles, stretching dough as needed and pressing firmly into bottoms and up sides of cups. Spoon filling into each cup, filling about three-fourths full.

5. Bake 30 to 35 minutes or until toothpick inserted into centers comes out clean. Cool in pan 15 minutes; remove to wire rack to cool completely.

Makes 12 mini pies

tip: If you don't have a 4-inch round cookie cutter, use the rim of a large mug to cut out circles of dough.

Chocolate Chip Cookie Mini Pies

Handheld Apple Pies

1 large Granny Smith apple, peeled and coarsely chopped
2 tablespoons sugar
1 teaspoon ground cinnamon
1 package (about 15 ounces) refrigerated pie crusts

1. Preheat oven to 350°F. Line large baking sheet with parchment paper. Combine sugar and cinnamon in small bowl.

2. Combine apple and half of cinnamon-sugar in medium bowl; toss to coat.

3. Unroll pie crusts on work surface. Cut out 12 circles with 4-inch round cookie cutter or small bowl. Reserve scraps of dough for decoration, if desired.

4. Place 1 dough circle on prepared baking sheet; brush edge of dough with water. Place generous tablespoon apple mixture on half of each dough circle, leaving ¼-inch border. Fold dough over filling, pressing lightly to seal. Dip fork in flour and crimp edges of dough to seal completely.

5. Cut out shapes from dough scraps with small cookie cutters, if desired; press onto tops of pies.

6. Bake 20 minutes or until crusts are golden brown. Sprinkle remaining cinnamon-sugar over hot pies. Serve warm. *Makes 12 servings*

Handheld Apple Pies

Chocolate Raspberry Chess Mini Pies

crust

- 1¼ cups all-purpose flour
- 1½ tablespoons sugar
- ½ teaspoon salt
- ¼ cup cold shortening, cubed
- 6 tablespoons (¾ stick) cold butter, cubed
- 4 tablespoons ice water

filling

- 4 squares (1 ounce each) unsweetened chocolate
- 3 tablespoons butter
- 3 eggs
- 1 egg yolk
- 1¼ cups sugar
- ½ cup half-and-half
- 2 teaspoons raspberry extract (optional)
- ¼ teaspoon salt
- Whipped cream and fresh raspberries (optional)

1. For crusts, combine flour, 1½ tablespoons sugar and ½ teaspoon salt in food processor; pulse to combine. Add shortening; pulse until blended. Add cold butter; pulse until mixture resembles coarse crumbs. Transfer to medium bowl. Sprinkle with water; use rubber spatula to fold in water until dough comes together. Shape dough into disc. Wrap in plastic wrap; refrigerate 1 hour.

2. For filling, heat chocolate and 3 tablespoons butter in small heavy saucepan over low heat until melted. Let stand 15 minutes. Whisk eggs and egg yolk in medium bowl. Whisk in 1¼ cups sugar, half-and-half, raspberry extract, if desired, and ¼ teaspoon salt until blended. Add chocolate mixture; stir until smooth.

3. Preheat oven to 350°F. Roll out dough to ⅛-inch thickness on floured surface (about 15×11-inch rectangle). Cut out circles with 4-inch round cookie cutter. Re-roll scraps of dough to cut out total of 12 circles.

4. Line 12 standard (2½-inch) muffin cups with dough circles, stretching dough as needed and pressing firmly into bottoms and up sides of cups. Spoon about ¼ cup filling into each crust.

5. Bake 20 to 25 minutes or until set. Cool in pan 10 minutes; remove to wire rack to cool completely. Refrigerate before serving. Garnish with whipped cream and raspberries.   *Makes 12 mini pies*

Chocolate Raspberry Chess Mini Pies

Apricot-Pecan Tartlets

crust

 1 cup all-purpose flour
 ½ cup (1 stick) cold butter, cut into pieces
 6 tablespoons cream cheese

filling

 ¾ cup packed light brown sugar
 1 egg
 1 tablespoon butter
 ½ teaspoon vanilla
 ¼ teaspoon salt
 ⅔ cup diced dried apricots
 ⅓ cup chopped pecans

1. For crusts, combine flour, cold butter and cream cheese in food processor; process with on/off pulses until mixture forms a ball. Wrap dough in plastic wrap; refrigerate 15 minutes.

2. Preheat oven to 325°F. Spray 24 mini (1¾-inch) muffin cups with nonstick cooking spray

3. For filling, beat brown sugar, egg, 1 tablespoon butter, vanilla and salt in large bowl with electric mixer at medium speed until creamy. Stir in apricots and pecans.

4. Shape dough into 24 balls; place in prepared muffin cups. Press dough into bottoms and up sides of prepared cups. Spoon about 1 teaspoon filling into each crust.

5. Bake 25 minutes or until light golden brown. Cool in pans on wire racks.

Makes 2 dozen tartlets

Apricot-Pecan Tartlets

Easy S'more Pies

¾ cup sour cream
6 mini graham cracker crusts
¾ cup milk chocolate chips
1½ cups mini marshmallows

1. Spread 2 tablespoons sour cream evenly in each crust. Sprinkle with 2 tablespoons chocolate chips and ¼ cup marshmallows.

2. Preheat grill to medium-low.

3. Place pies on grill; cover with 13×9-inch metal baking pan. Grill 5 minutes or until marshmallows and chocolate are melted, checking frequently. Serve immediately. *Makes 6 servings*

tip

If you're not lighting your grill for dinner, you can use your oven for these pies instead. Simply bake them in a preheated 350°F oven for 3 to 5 minutes or until the marshmallows and chocolate are melted.

Easy S'more Pies

Maple Walnut Mini Pies

crust

- 1¼ cups all-purpose flour
- 1½ tablespoons granulated sugar
- ½ teaspoon salt
- ¼ cup cold shortening, cubed
- 6 tablespoons (¾ stick) cold butter, cubed
- 4 tablespoons ice water

filling

- 1 cup maple syrup
- 3 eggs
- ½ cup packed dark brown sugar
- 1 tablespoon butter, melted
- 1 teaspoon vanilla
- ¼ teaspoon salt
- 1 cup coarsely chopped walnuts

1. For crusts, combine 1¼ cups flour, 1½ tablespoons granulated sugar and ½ teaspoon salt in food processor; pulse to combine. Add shortening; pulse until blended. Add cold butter; pulse until mixture forms coarse crumbs. Transfer to medium bowl. Sprinkle with water; use rubber spatula to fold in water until dough comes together. Shape dough into disc. Wrap in plastic wrap; refrigerate 1 hour.

2. For filling, beat maple syrup, eggs, brown sugar, melted butter, vanilla and ¼ teaspoon salt in large bowl with electric mixer at medium speed until well blended. Stir in walnuts.

3. Preheat oven to 350°F. Roll out dough to ⅛-inch thickness on floured surface (about 15×11-inch rectangle). Cut out circles with 4-inch round cookie cutter. Re-roll scraps of dough to cut out total of 12 circles.

4. Line 12 standard (2½-inch) muffin cups with dough circles, stretching dough as needed and pressing firmly into bottoms and up sides of cups. Spoon about ¼ cup filling into each cup.

5. Bake 20 to 25 minutes or until center is set. Cool in pan 15 minutes; remove to wire rack to cool completely. *Makes 12 mini pies*

Maple Walnut Mini Pies

Chocolate Tartlets

crust

>   2 cups all-purpose flour
>   1 cup (2 sticks) cold butter, cubed
>   2 packages (3 ounces each) cold cream cheese, cut into chunks

filling

>   2 tablespoons butter
>   2 squares (1 ounce each) unsweetened chocolate
>   1½ cups packed brown sugar
>   2 eggs, beaten
>   2 teaspoons vanilla
>   ⅛ teaspoon salt
>   1½ cups chopped pecans

1. For crusts, place flour in large bowl. Cut in cold butter and cream cheese with pastry blender or two knives; mix until dough can be shaped into a ball. Wrap in plastic wrap; refrigerate 1 hour.

2. Shape dough into 1-inch balls. Place in 60 mini (1¾-inch) muffin cups, pressing into bottoms and up sides of cups. Refrigerate while preparing filling. Preheat oven to 350°F.

3. For filling, melt 2 tablespoons butter and chocolate in medium heavy saucepan over low heat. Remove from heat; stir in brown sugar, eggs, vanilla and salt until well blended and thick. Stir in pecans. Spoon about 1 teaspoon filling into each crust.

4. Bake 20 to 25 minutes or until filling is set and crusts are lightly browned. Cool in pans on wire racks.   *Makes 5 dozen tartlets*

Chocolate Tartlets

tiny tarts

Figgy Tarts

Basic Short Dough (page 107)
1½ cups finely chopped dried figs
½ cup orange juice
¼ cup light corn syrup
2 tablespoons packed brown sugar
2 tablespoons grated orange peel
¼ teaspoon ground cinnamon
Pinch ground cloves
Orange peel strips (optional)

1. Prepare Basic Short Dough. Divide dough into two discs. Wrap discs in plastic wrap. Refrigerate at least 1 hour or until firm.

2. For filling, combine figs, orange juice, corn syrup, brown sugar, orange peel, cinnamon and cloves in medium saucepan; cook and stir over low heat 4 to 5 minutes or until figs are softened. Set aside to cool.

3. Let dough stand at room temperature 5 minutes. Lightly spray 48 mini (1¾-inch) muffin cups with nonstick cooking spray.

4. Roll out half of dough to ⅛-inch thickness on lightly floured surface. Cut out circles with 2½-inch fluted round cookie cutter. Place in prepared muffin cups, pressing dough into bottoms and up sides of cups and sealing any cracks. Repeat with remaining dough. Re-roll dough scraps once. Refrigerate at least 30 minutes before baking.

5. Preheat oven to 375°F. Prick holes in bottom of each crust with fork. Bake 10 to 12 minutes or until golden brown. Cool in pans on wire racks 10 minutes.

6. Spoon about 1 tablespoon filling into each crust; refrigerate until ready to serve. Garnish with orange peel. *Makes 4 dozen tarts*

Key Lime Tarts

¾ cup milk

6 tablespoons fresh lime juice

2 tablespoons cornstarch

2 eggs

½ cup sugar

½ cup sour cream

4 sheets phyllo dough

Fresh raspberries and lime slices (optional)

1. For filling, combine milk, lime juice and cornstarch in medium saucepan. Cook over medium heat 2 to 3 minutes or until thickened, stirring constantly. Remove from heat.

2. Add eggs; whisk constantly 30 seconds. Stir in sugar and sour cream until blended. Cover and refrigerate until cool.

3. For crusts, preheat oven to 350°F. Spray 8 standard (2½-inch) muffin cups with butter-flavored cooking spray.

4. Place 1 sheet of phyllo dough on work surface; spray lightly with cooking spray. Layer with remaining 3 sheets phyllo dough, lightly spraying each sheet with cooking spray.

5. Cut stack of phyllo dough into 8 squares. Gently place phyllo stacks in prepared muffin cups; press firmly into bottoms and up sides of cups.

6. Bake 8 to 10 minutes or until golden brown. Remove from muffin cups; cool on wire rack.

7. Divide filling evenly among phyllo cups. Garnish with raspberries and lime slices. *Makes 8 tarts*

Key Lime Tart

Portuguese Cream Tarts

1 cup granulated sugar
2 tablespoons all-purpose flour
2½ cups whipping cream
8 egg yolks
    Finely grated peel of 1 lemon (about 1¼ teaspoons)
1 teaspoon vanilla
¼ teaspoon salt
1 tablespoon butter, melted
1 package (about 17 ounces) frozen puff pastry, partially thawed
    (dough should be stiff)
    Powdered sugar (optional)

1. For filling, whisk granulated sugar and flour in medium heavy saucepan. Whisk in cream, egg yolks, lemon peel, vanilla and salt until smooth. Cook over medium heat about 10 minutes or until mixture thickens and begins to bubble, whisking constantly. Transfer to medium bowl; cool about 15 minutes, whisking occasionally.

2. For crusts, preheat oven to 450°F. Brush 24 mini (1¾-inch) muffin cups with melted butter. Unfold 1 sheet puff pastry on work surface; cut into three strips along folds. Stack pieces; cut lengthwise into 12 (¼-inch-wide) strips. Repeat with remaining sheet of puff pastry.

3. Turn each triple strip on its side, cut side up, and coil tightly into flat 2-inch-wide spiral. Place on lightly floured surface; press spiral with hand to flatten into 3-inch round.

4. Place puff pastry rounds in prepared muffin cups, pressing gently into bottoms and up sides of cups. Spoon about 2 tablespoons filling into each crust.

5. Bake 10 to 12 minutes or until crusts are golden brown. Cool in pans 10 minutes; remove to wire racks. Serve warm or at room temperature. Sprinkle with powdered sugar, if desired.   *Makes 2 dozen tarts*

Portuguese Cream Tarts

Raspberry Almond Tarts

crust

>   **Basic Short Dough (page 107)**
> ½ **teaspoon almond extract**

filling

>   1 **can or tube (8 ounces) almond paste (do not use marzipan)**
> ¼ **cup sugar**
>   2 **eggs**
> ¼ **cup seedless raspberry jam**
>   **Sliced almonds (optional)**

1. For crusts, prepare Basic Short Dough, substituting almond extract for vanilla. Divide dough into two discs; wrap in plastic wrap. Refrigerate at least 1 hour or until firm.

2. Preheat oven to 350°F. Let dough stand at room temperature 5 minutes. Lightly spray 48 mini (1¾-inch) muffin cups with nonstick cooking spray.

3. Roll out half of dough to ⅛-inch thickness on lightly floured surface. Cut out circles with 2½-inch fluted round cookie cutter. Place in prepared muffin cups, pressing dough into bottom and up sides of cups and sealing any cracks. Repeat with remaining dough. Re-roll dough scraps once.

4. For filling, beat almond paste and sugar in medium bowl until blended. Add eggs, one at a time; beat until well blended. Spoon about 1 teaspoon filling into each crust.

5. Bake 18 to 20 minutes or until lightly browned. Cool completely in pans on wire racks.

6. Just before serving, spoon ½ teaspoon jam on each tart. Garnish with sliced almond.   *Makes 4 dozen tarts*

Raspberry Almond Tarts

Black Forest Tarts

1 package (about 16 ounces) refrigerated triple chocolate
    cookie dough
⅓ cup unsweetened cocoa powder
1 can (21 ounces) cherry pie filling
3 squares (1 ounce each) white chocolate, finely chopped

1. For crusts, preheat oven to 350°F. Line 18 standard (2½-inch) muffin cups with foil or paper baking cups or lightly spray with nonstick cooking spray. Let dough stand at room temperature 15 minutes.

2. Beat dough and cocoa in large bowl until well blended. Shape dough into 18 balls; press into bottoms and up sides of prepared muffin cups.

3. Bake about 15 minutes or until set. Gently press down center of each crust with back of teaspoon. Cool in pans 10 minutes; remove to wire racks to cool completely.

4. Spoon 1 tablespoon cherry pie filling into each crust. Place white chocolate in small resealable food storage bag. Microwave on MEDIUM (50%) 1 minute; knead bag lightly. Microwave and knead at additional 30-second intervals until chocolate is completely melted. Cut off small corner of bag; drizzle chocolate over tarts. Let stand until set.

Makes 1½ dozen tarts

tip

If triple chocolate cookie dough is not available, you
can use plain sugar cookie dough and add extra cocoa
powder instead. Use ½ cup cocoa instead of ⅓ cup,
and proceed with the recipe as directed in Step 2.

Black Forest Tart

Apricot Tartlets

4 sheets frozen phyllo dough, thawed
1 can (15 ounces) apricot halves in juice, drained
4 tablespoons apricot preserves, divided
1 tablespoon powdered sugar
1 teaspoon ground cinnamon

1. Preheat oven to 350°F. Line baking sheet with foil; spray foil with butter-flavored cooking spray.

2. Place 1 sheet of phyllo dough on work surface; keep remaining sheets covered with plastic wrap and damp towel. Spray phyllo dough with cooking spray. Fold in half to create 8×6-inch rectangle; spray with cooking spray.

3. Place 3 apricot halves, cut side up, in center of phyllo dough. Spread with 1 tablespoon preserves. Fold and pleat about 1 inch of dough around edges to form round tartlet crust. Repeat with remaining phyllo dough, apricots and preserves.

4. Bake 22 minutes or until phyllo is golden brown and crisp. Combine powdered sugar and cinnamon in small bowl; sprinkle over tartlets. Serve warm. *Makes 4 tartlets*

tip

Phyllo dough dries out very quickly and crumbles easily.
Keep thawed phyllo dough wrapped or covered until
all the ingredients are assembled and you are ready
to work with the dough.

Apricot Tartlets

Mini Pecan Tarts

crust

> 2 cups all-purpose flour
> 1 teaspoon granulated sugar
> ⅛ teaspoon salt
> ¾ cup (1½ sticks) cold butter, cut into pieces
> 5 tablespoons ice water

filling

> 1 cup powdered sugar
> ½ cup (1 stick) butter
> ⅓ cup dark corn syrup
> 1 cup chopped pecans
> 36 pecan halves

1. For crusts, combine flour, granulated sugar and salt in large bowl. Cut in cold butter with pastry blender or two knives until mixture resembles coarse crumbs. Add water, 1 tablespoon at a time, kneading until dough forms a ball. Shape dough into disc; wrap in plastic wrap. Refrigerate at least 30 minutes.

2. Preheat oven to 375°F. Spray 36 mini (1¾-inch) muffin cups with nonstick cooking spray. Roll out dough to ⅛-inch thickness on lightly floured surface. Cut out circles with 2½-inch round cookie cutter; press into prepared muffin cups.

3. Bake 8 minutes or until very lightly browned. *Reduce oven temperature to 350°F.*

4. For filling, combine powdered sugar, ½ cup butter and corn syrup in medium saucepan. Cook over medium heat 4 to 5 minutes or until mixture comes to a full boil, stirring occasionally. Remove from heat; stir in chopped pecans.

5. Spoon filling evenly into warm baked crusts; top each with pecan half. Bake 5 minutes. Cool completely in pans on wire racks.

Makes 3 dozen tarts

Mini Pecan Tarts

Cherry Berry Heart Tarts

1 can (14½ ounces) red tart cherries in water
¾ cup plus 1 tablespoon sugar, divided
2 tablespoons cornstarch
¼ teaspoon salt
1 teaspoon lemon juice
1 cup frozen raspberries (not in syrup), thawed and drained
1 package (about 15 ounces) refrigerated pie crusts
2 tablespoons milk

1. For filling, drain cherries, reserving liquid. Combine ¾ cup sugar, cornstarch and salt in medium saucepan. Stir in ⅓ cup cherry liquid and lemon juice until blended. Stir in cherries; bring to a simmer over medium heat. Cook and stir about 6 minutes or until thickened. Gently stir in raspberries; set aside to cool.

2. For crusts, preheat oven to 400°F. Line small cookie sheet with parchment paper. Unroll pie crusts on work surface; cut out 20 circles with 3-inch round cookie cutter. Cut out 20 hearts from dough scraps with ½-inch heart-shaped cookie cutter.*

3. Place heart cutouts on prepared cookie sheet. Brush with milk; sprinkle with remaining 1 tablespoon sugar. Bake about 7 minutes or until golden brown. Remove to wire rack to cool.

4. Press dough circles into 20 mini (1¾-inch) muffin cups and flute edges. Spoon about 1 tablespoon filling into each crust.

5. Bake 15 minutes or until crusts are golden brown and filling is bubbly. Cool tarts in pans 5 minutes; remove to wire racks to cool completely. Place one heart cutout in center of each tart. *Makes 20 tarts*

If you don't have a small heart-shaped cookie cutter, you can cut out the hearts with scissors.

Cherry Berry Heart Tarts

Chocolate Cappuccino Tarts

crust

> **Basic Chocolate Short Dough (page 107)**
> **1 teaspoon instant coffee granules**

filling

> **4 ounces cream cheese, softened**
> **½ cup sweetened condensed milk**
> **1 egg**
> **½ teaspoon instant coffee granules**
> **½ (8-ounce) container thawed frozen whipped topping**
> **Ground cinnamon**
> **Chocolate-covered coffee beans (optional)**

1. For crusts, prepare Basic Chocolate Short Dough, adding 1 teaspoon instant coffee granules to butter and sugar mixture. Divide dough into two discs; wrap in plastic wrap. Refrigerate at least 1 hour or until firm.

2. Let dough stand at room temperature 5 minutes. Lightly spray 48 mini (1¾-inch) muffin cups with nonstick cooking spray.

3. Roll out half of dough to ⅛-inch thickness on lightly floured surface. Cut out circles with 2½-inch fluted round cookie cutter. Place in prepared muffin cups, pressing dough into bottom and up sides of cups and sealing any cracks. Repeat with remaining dough. Re-roll dough scraps once. Refrigerate at least 30 minutes.

4. Preheat oven to 350°F. Prick holes in bottom of each crust with fork. Bake 8 minutes.

5. For filling, beat cream cheese and sweetened condensed milk in medium bowl with electric mixer at medium speed until smooth. Beat in egg and ½ teaspoon instant coffee granules until well blended. Pour filling evenly into crusts.

6. Bake 6 to 8 minutes or until filling is set. Cool completely in pans on wire racks. Refrigerate until ready to serve. Top each tart with whipped topping; sprinkle with cinnamon. Garnish with chocolate-covered coffee bean.   *Makes 4 dozen tarts*

Chocolate Cappuccino Tarts

Apricot and Toasted Almond Tarts

½ cup cottage cheese
4 ounces cream cheese, softened
1 tablespoon milk
4 teaspoons sugar
¼ teaspoon vanilla
4 sheets frozen phyllo dough, thawed
3 tablespoons apricot or blackberry preserves
¼ cup sliced almonds, toasted*

To toast almonds, spread in single layer on baking sheet. Bake in preheated 350°F oven 6 to 8 minutes or until golden brown, stirring frequently.

1. Preheat oven to 350°F. Spray 8 standard (2½-inch) muffin cups with butter-flavored cooking spray.

2. Beat cottage cheese, cream cheese, milk, sugar and vanilla in medium bowl with electric mixer at high speed until completely smooth. Refrigerate until ready to use.

3. Place 1 sheet of phyllo dough on work surface; spray lightly with cooking spray. Layer with remaining 3 sheets phyllo dough, lightly spraying each sheet with cooking spray.

4. Cut stack of phyllo dough into 8 squares. Gently place phyllo stacks in prepared muffin cups; press firmly into bottoms and up sides of cups.

5. Bake 5 minutes or until golden brown. Cool in pan on wire rack.

6. Place preserves in small microwavable bowl; microwave on HIGH 20 seconds or just until melted. Spoon 2 tablespoons cream cheese mixture into each crust; drizzle with 1 teaspoon melted preserves. Sprinkle with almonds.

Makes 8 tarts

Apricot and Toasted Almond Tarts

Mincemeat Tartlets

crust

2½ cups all purpose flour

9 tablespoons powdered sugar

3½ teaspoons grated orange peel

½ teaspoon salt

¾ cup (1½ sticks) cold butter, cut into ½-inch pieces

2 egg yolks

2 to 3 tablespoons orange juice

filling

1½ cups prepared mincemeat

½ cup chopped peeled tart apple

⅓ cup golden raisins

⅓ cup chopped walnuts

3 tablespoons brandy

1 tablespoon grated orange peel

1 egg, beaten

1. For crusts, combine flour, powdered sugar, 3½ teaspoons orange peel and salt in food processor; pulse to combine. Add butter; pulse until mixture resembles coarse crumbs. Whisk egg yolks and 2 tablespoons orange juice in small bowl. Pour over flour mixture; pulse until moist clumps form. If dough is too dry, add additional orange juice, 1 teaspoon at a time. Shape dough into disc. Wrap in plastic wrap; refrigerate 30 minutes.

2. For filling, combine mincemeat, apple, raisins, walnuts, brandy and 1 tablespoon orange peel in medium bowl until well blended.

3. Preheat oven to 375°F. Spray 36 mini (1¾-inch) muffin cups with nonstick cooking spray. Remove two thirds of dough from refrigerator; roll into ⅛-inch-thick circle on lightly floured surface. Cut out 36 circles with 2½- to 3-inch round cookie cutter, re-rolling dough scraps as necessary.

4. Press dough circles into prepared muffin cups. Spoon about 1 tablespoon filling into each crust.

5. Roll out remaining third of dough into ⅛-inch-thick circle on lightly floured surface. Cut out 36 circles with 2-inch round cookie cutter, re-rolling dough scraps as necessary.

6. Brush dough circles with beaten egg; place over filling, egg side down. Press edges of dough to seal. Cut slits or decorative designs in tops for steam to escape. Brush tops with beaten egg.

7. Bake about 20 minutes or until crusts are golden brown. Cool in pans 5 minutes. Cut around edges of tartlets with small knife to loosen; remove to wire racks to cool. Serve warm or at room temperature.

Makes 36 tartlets

Mincemeat Tartlets

Quick Chocolate Fruit Tarts

1 refrigerated pie crust (half of 15-ounce package)
1¼ cups prepared chocolate pudding (about 4 snack-size cups)
Fresh sliced strawberries, raspberries, blackberries or favorite fruit

1. Preheat oven to 450°F. Spray back of standard (2½-inch) 12-cup muffin pan with nonstick cooking spray. Let pie crust stand at room temperature 15 minutes.

2. Unroll crust on work surface; cut out 6 circles with 4-inch round cookie cutter. Place dough circles over backs of alternating muffin cups, pleating around sides of cups. (Press firmly to hold dough in place.) Prick bottom and sides with fork.

3. Bake about 8 minutes or until golden brown. Carefully remove tart shells from backs of muffin cups; cool completely on wire rack.

4. Fill each tart shell with about 3 tablespoons pudding; arrange fruit over pudding. *Makes 6 tarts*

Lemon Mini Tarts

½ cup powdered sugar
2 egg yolks
3 tablespoons butter, melted
2 tablespoons freshly squeezed lemon juice
1 tablespoon lemon peel
1 tablespoon granulated sugar
24 mini frozen phyllo shells*
Mint leaves (optional)
Raspberries (optional)

Frozen phyllo shells can be found in the freezer section by the other frozen hors d'oeuvres.

1. Preheat oven to 350°F. Whisk powdered sugar, egg yolks, butter, lemon juice, lemon peel and granulated sugar in small bowl until well blended.

2. Spoon 1 teaspoon filling into each frozen phyllo shell.

3. Bake 13 to 15 minutes or until centers are set. Garnish with mint and raspberries. *Makes 2 dozen tarts*

Basic Short Dough

 2 cups all-purpose flour
 ¼ teaspoon salt
 ¾ cup (1½ sticks) butter, slightly softened
 ¾ cup sugar
 3 egg yolks
 1 teaspoon vanilla

1. Sift flour and salt into medium bowl. Beat butter and sugar in large bowl with electric mixer at medium speed 1 minute. Beat in egg yolks and vanilla until well blended. Add flour mixture; beat just until combined.

2. Shape dough into two discs. Wrap in plastic wrap; refrigerate 1 hour or up to 3 days. Dough may be frozen up to 1 month.

Basic Chocolate Short Dough

 1½ cups all-purpose flour
 ¼ cup unsweetened Dutch process cocoa powder*
 ¼ teaspoon salt
 ¾ cup (1½ sticks) butter, slightly softened
 ¾ cup sugar
 3 egg yolks
 1 teaspoon vanilla

Natural unsweetened cocoa powder may be substituted. Dutch process cocoa powder is darker in color and has a stronger flavor.

1. Sift flour, cocoa and salt into medium bowl. Beat butter and sugar in large bowl with electric mixer at medium speed 1 minute. Beat in egg yolks and vanilla until well blended. Add flour mixture; beat just until combined.

2. Shape dough into two discs. Wrap in plastic wrap; refrigerate 1 hour or up to 3 days. Dough may be frozen up to 1 month.

Plum-Topped Custard Tartlets

1 cup half-and-half
2 eggs
½ cup plus 1 tablespoon granulated sugar, divided
1 tablespoon all-purpose flour
½ teaspoon vanilla
½ cup cold whipping cream
1 package (10 ounces) frozen puff pastry shells (6 shells), baked according to package directions
1 tablespoon butter
2 large firm red plums, unpeeled, cut into thin wedges
1 tablespoon packed brown sugar

1. For filling, bring half-and-half to a simmer in medium saucepan over medium heat. Beat eggs, ½ cup granulated sugar and flour in medium bowl. Gradually pour about ½ cup hot half-and-half into egg mixture, stirring constantly. Pour egg mixture back into saucepan; cook over medium-low heat 7 to 8 minutes or until mixture thickens, stirring constantly.

2. Remove from heat; stir in vanilla. Pour through fine-mesh strainer into bowl. Chill custard until thick and cold.

3. Beat cream in large bowl with electric mixer at medium-high speed until soft peaks form. Add remaining 1 tablespoon granulated sugar; beat at high speed until stiff peaks form. Fold chilled custard into whipped cream.

4. Spoon about ¼ cup filling into each pastry shell. Refrigerate any remaining custard.

5. Melt butter in medium skillet over medium-high heat. Add plums; cook 2 minutes or until plums become slightly softened. Stir in brown sugar; cook and stir 1 minute or until plums are glazed.

6. Spoon plums over custard filling. Serve immediately.

Makes 6 tartlets

Cranberry Phyllo Cheesecake Tarts

1 cup fresh or frozen cranberries
¼ cup plus 1 tablespoon sugar, divided
2 tablespoons orange juice
1 teaspoon grated orange peel
¼ teaspoon ground allspice
6 sheets phyllo dough, thawed
1 container (8 ounces) whipped cream cheese
8 ounces vanilla yogurt
1 teaspoon vanilla

1. Preheat oven to 350°F. Lightly spray 12 standard (2½-inch) muffin cups with butter-flavored cooking spray.

2. For topping, combine cranberries, ¼ cup sugar, orange juice, orange peel and allspice in small saucepan; cook and stir over medium heat until berries pop and mixture thickens. Set aside to cool completely.

3. For crusts, cut phyllo sheets in half lengthwise, then crosswise into thirds. Spray 1 phyllo square lightly with cooking spray. Top with second square, slightly offsetting corners; spray lightly with cooking spray. Top with third square. Place phyllo stack in prepared muffin cup, pressing into bottom and up side of cup. Repeat with remaining phyllo squares.

4. Bake 3 to 4 minutes or until golden brown. Cool completely in pan on wire rack.

5. For filling, beat cream cheese, yogurt, remaining 1 tablespoon sugar and vanilla in medium bowl with electric mixer at medium speed until smooth. Spoon filling evenly into crusts; top with cranberry mixture.

Makes 12 tarts

Cranberry Phyllo Cheesecake Tart

Elegant Lace Cookie Cups

½ cup light corn syrup
½ cup (1 stick) butter
1 cup all-purpose flour
½ cup slivered almonds, finely chopped
¼ cup granulated sugar
¼ cup packed brown sugar
2 tablespoons whipping cream
Ice cream
Melted semisweet chocolate (optional)

1. Preheat oven to 300°F. Line cookie sheets with parchment paper.

2. Bring corn syrup to a boil in medium saucepan over medium heat. Add butter; cook and stir over low heat 2 to 3 minutes or until butter is melted. Remove from heat; stir in flour, almonds, granulated sugar, brown sugar and cream until blended. Drop tablespoonfuls of batter 4 inches apart onto prepared cookie sheets.

3. Bake 11 to 13 minutes or until cookies are bubbly and golden brown. Cool 30 seconds on cookie sheets.

4. Working quickly, shape cookies over inverted custard cups or ramekins to form cups. Cool completely.

5. Just before serving, fill each cookie cup with scoop of ice cream. Drizzle with melted chocolate, if desired.   *Makes 2 dozen cookie cups*

Tip: If you don't need all 24 cookie cups, just make the desired number of cups. Bake the remaining batter as directed above but leave the cookies flat; cool on cookie sheets 30 seconds, then remove to wire racks to cool completely.

Elegant Lace Cookie Cup

Mini Chocolate Cheesecakes

8 squares (1 ounce each) semisweet baking chocolate, chopped
3 packages (8 ounces each) cream cheese, softened
½ cup sugar
3 eggs
1 teaspoon vanilla

1. Preheat oven to 325°F. Lightly spray 12 standard (2½-inch) muffin cups with nonstick cooking spray.

2. Place chocolate in 1-cup microwavable bowl. Microwave on HIGH 1 to 1½ minutes or until chocolate is melted, stirring after 1 minute. Let cool slightly.

3. Beat cream cheese and sugar in large bowl with electric mixer at medium speed about 2 minutes or until light and fluffy. Add eggs and vanilla; beat about 2 minutes or until well blended. Beat melted chocolate into cream cheese mixture until well blended.

4. Divide mixture evenly among prepared muffin cups. Place muffin pan in larger baking pan; place on oven rack. Pour warm water into larger pan to depth of ½ to 1 inch.

5. Bake 30 minutes or until edges are dry and centers are almost set. Remove muffin pan from water. Cool completely in pan on wire rack.

Makes 12 cheesecakes

mini swirl cheesecakes: Before adding chocolate to cream cheese mixture, place about 2 heaping tablespoons of plain mixture in each muffin cup. Add chocolate to remaining cream cheese mixture in bowl; beat until well blended. Spoon chocolate mixture on top of plain mixture in muffin cups; swirl with knife before baking.

Mini Swirl Cheesecakes

Tiny Hot Fudge Sundae Cups

1 package (about 16 ounces) refrigerated sugar cookie dough

⅓ cup unsweetened cocoa powder

5 to 7 cups vanilla ice cream

Hot fudge ice cream topping, colored sprinkles and whipped cream

9 maraschino cherries, cut into quarters

1. Let dough stand at room temperature 15 minutes. Spray backs of 36 mini (1¾-inch) muffin cups with nonstick cooking spray.

2. Preheat oven to 350°F. Beat dough and cocoa in large bowl with electric mixer at medium speed until well blended. Divide dough into 36 equal pieces; shape each piece over back of prepared muffin cup.

3. Bake 10 to 12 minutes or until set. Cool in pans 10 minutes; remove to wire racks to cool completely.

4. Fill each cup with ice cream. Drizzle with hot fudge topping; top with sprinkles. Garnish each sundae with whipped cream and cherry quarter. Serve immediately. *Makes 3 dozen sundae cups*

tip

To fill the chocolate cups, use a cookie scoop or melon baller to get the perfect size scoops of ice cream. A standard ice cream scoop is too big for this job.

Tiny Hot Fudge Sundae Cups

Cherry Hand Pies

1 can (21 ounces) cherry pie filling
2 teaspoons grated orange peel
1 package (about 15 ounces) refrigerated pie crusts
1 egg yolk
1 tablespoon milk
1 tablespoon sugar
½ teaspoon ground cinnamon
   4-inch round cookie cutter

1. Preheat oven to 375°F. Line large baking sheet with parchment paper. Combine pie filling and orange peel in medium bowl.

2. Roll out 1 pie crust into 12-inch circle on lightly floured surface. Cut out 6 circles with 4-inch round cookie cutter. Repeat with second crust.

3. Beat egg yolk and milk in small bowl until blended. Combine sugar and cinnamon in separate small bowl.

4. Spoon scant tablespoon filling in center of each dough circle, leaving ¼-inch border. Brush edges of circles with egg yolk mixture. Fold dough over filling, pressing lightly to seal. Crimp edges of dough with fork to seal completely. Place on prepared baking sheet.

5. Cut slits in tops of pies with paring knife. Brush with remaining egg yolk mixture; sprinkle with cinnamon-sugar.

6. Bake 18 to 20 minutes or until golden brown. Remove to wire rack to cool slightly. Serve warm. *Makes 12 hand pies*

Cherry Hand Pie

Peanutty Crispy Dessert Cups

⅓ cup creamy peanut butter
2 tablespoons butter
3 cups standard marshmallows (5 ounces)
3 cups chocolate-flavored crisp rice cereal
　Ice cream or frozen yogurt
　Chocolate sauce, colored candies and sprinkles, chopped
　　peanuts, strawberries and/or maraschino cherries

1. Heat peanut butter and butter in large saucepan over low heat until melted and smooth. Add marshmallows; cook until melted, stirring constantly. Remove pan from heat; stir in cereal until well blended and cooled slightly.

2. Scoop mixture evenly into 12 standard (2½-inch) nonstick muffin cups; press into bottoms and up sides of cups.

3. Refrigerate 5 to 10 minutes or until set. Remove cups from pan; fill with ice cream and sprinkle with desired toppings. *Makes 12 cups*

Candy Cups

1 package (about 16 ounces) refrigerated sugar cookie dough
⅓ cup all-purpose flour
1 package (12 ounces) bite-size chocolate-covered peanut,
　　caramel and nougat candy
¼ cup cocktail peanuts, chopped

1. Preheat oven to 350°F. Lightly spray 36 mini (1¾-inch) muffin cups with nonstick spray. Let dough stand at room temperature 15 minutes.

2. Beat dough and flour in large bowl until well blended. Shape dough into 36 balls; press into bottoms and up sides of prepared muffin cups. Place 1 candy into center of each cup.

3. Bake 10 to 11 minutes or until edges are golden brown. Immediately sprinkle with peanuts. Cool in pans 10 minutes; remove to wire racks to cool completely. *Makes 3 dozen cups*

Peanutty Crispy Dessert Cups

Coconut Craters

1 package (about 16 ounces) refrigerated chocolate chip cookie dough
¼ cup packed brown sugar
2 tablespoons milk
1 tablespoon butter, melted
1 cup flaked coconut
½ cup chocolate-covered toffee baking bits

1. Preheat oven to 350°F. Line 36 mini (1¾-inch) muffin cups with paper baking cups or spray with nonstick cooking spray. Let dough stand at room temperature 15 minutes.

2. Shape dough into 36 balls; press into bottoms and up sides of prepared muffin cups. Bake 9 to 11 minutes or until golden brown. Gently press down center of each cookie cup with back of teaspoon.

3. For filling, whisk brown sugar, milk and butter in medium bowl until blended. Stir in coconut and toffee bits. Spoon 1 rounded teaspoon toffee mixture into each cup.

4. Bake 2 to 4 minutes or until golden brown. Cool in pan 10 minutes; remove to wire racks to cool completely. *Makes 3 dozen tarts*

Coconut Craters

Chocolate Mousse Phyllo Tarts

  8 sheets frozen phyllo dough, thawed
½ cup semisweet chocolate chips, divided
⅔ cup cold whipping cream
  1 tablespoon powdered sugar
½ teaspoon vanilla
  3 tablespoons seedless raspberry preserves
     Fresh raspberries and fresh mint leaves (optional)

1. Preheat oven to 350°F. Spray 8 standard (2½-inch) muffin cups with butter-flavored cooking spray.

2. For crusts, place large piece of parchment or waxed paper on work surface. Place 1 sheet of phyllo dough on parchment paper; keep remaining sheets covered with plastic wrap and damp towels. Spray phyllo dough lightly with cooking spray; cut into 4 squares. Stack squares, sprayed sides down, in prepared muffin cup, pressing into bottom and up side of cup. Spray top square with cooking spray. Repeat with remaining phyllo.

3. Bake 5 to 6 minutes or until golden brown. Cool completely in pan on wire rack.

4. For filling, place ¼ cup chocolate chips in medium microwavable bowl. Microwave on MEDIUM (50%) 1 minute. Stir; microwave at 10-second intervals, if necessary, until melted and smooth.

5. Beat cream in medium bowl with electric mixer at medium speed until soft peaks form. Beat in powdered sugar and vanilla until blended. Fold in melted chocolate until well blended.

6. Spoon about 1 teaspoon preserves in bottom of each crust; top with ¼ cup chocolate mousse. Cover and refrigerate until ready to serve.

7. Sprinkle with remaining ¼ cup chocolate chips. Garnish with raspberries and mint.   *Makes 8 tarts*

Chocolate Mousse Phyllo Tart

metric conversion chart

VOLUME MEASUREMENTS (dry)

1/8 teaspoon = 0.5 mL
1/4 teaspoon = 1 mL
1/2 teaspoon = 2 mL
3/4 teaspoon = 4 mL
1 teaspoon = 5 mL
1 tablespoon = 15 mL
2 tablespoons = 30 mL
1/4 cup = 60 mL
1/3 cup = 75 mL
1/2 cup = 125 mL
2/3 cup = 150 mL
3/4 cup = 175 mL
1 cup = 250 mL
2 cups = 1 pint = 500 mL
3 cups = 750 mL
4 cups = 1 quart = 1 L

VOLUME MEASUREMENTS (fluid)

1 fluid ounce (2 tablespoons) = 30 mL
4 fluid ounces (1/2 cup) = 125 mL
8 fluid ounces (1 cup) = 250 mL
12 fluid ounces (11/2 cups) = 375 mL
16 fluid ounces (2 cups) = 500 mL

WEIGHTS (mass)

1/2 ounce = 15 g
1 ounce = 30 g
3 ounces = 90 g
4 ounces = 120 g
8 ounces = 225 g
10 ounces = 285 g
12 ounces = 360 g
16 ounces = 1 pound = 450 g

DIMENSIONS

1/16 inch = 2 mm
1/8 inch = 3 mm
1/4 inch = 6 mm
1/2 inch = 1.5 cm
3/4 inch = 2 cm
1 inch = 2.5 cm

OVEN TEMPERATURES

250°F = 120°C
275°F = 140°C
300°F = 150°C
325°F = 160°C
350°F = 180°C
375°F = 190°C
400°F = 200°C
425°F = 220°C
450°F = 230°C

BAKING PAN SIZES

Utensil	Size in Inches/Quarts	Metric Volume	Size in Centimeters
Baking or Cake Pan (square or rectangular)	8×8×2	2 L	20×20×5
	9×9×2	2.5 L	23×23×5
	12×8×2	3 L	30×20×5
	13×9×2	3.5 L	33×23×5
Loaf Pan	8×4×3	1.5 L	20×10×7
	9×5×3	2 L	23×13×7
Round Layer Cake Pan	8×1½	1.2 L	20×4
	9×1½	1.5 L	23×4
Pie Plate	8×1¼	750 mL	20×3
	9×1¼	1 L	23×3
Baking Dish or Casserole	1 quart	1 L	—
	1½ quart	1.5 L	—
	2 quart	2 L	—